How To Back-Up a Tractor-Trailer SAFELY

All illustrations by Jerry Berger

This book has been written, distributed and sold with the intent of providing basic information in order to educate and enlighten the reader to utilize the basic advice and generally accepted concepts used by professional tractor-trailer drivers. The reader, and every driver, regardless of the vehicle being driven, has the sole responsibility to operate their vehicle in a safe and compliant manner as written under the jurisdiction of Federal, State and Local motor vehicle laws.

Information for CPSIA laws can be found at www.IGCtesting.com

Website: *www.HowToBackupATractorTrailerSafely.com*
To order this book in single or bulk quantities please call toll free: 1-877-587-3177

ISBN: 978-0-9899452-0-2 (Perfect Bound)

Printed in the U.S.A. by NJB Publishing Company

About the Author

Jerry Berger has worn three different "hats" within the industry: As an OTR (over-the-road) professional driver, Jerry has driven forty eight-states plus Canada. His driver duties also included the additional responsibility of training new drivers starting within the industry.

After leaving the road his occupational duties changed to that of Safety Director, working for two national trucking companies that ran freight, refrigerated and dry, throughout the United States and Canada.

The third aspect of Mr. Berger's career in the transportation industry has been as a Certified Commercial Driving School Instructor, teaching all driving and backing-up skills required of the trucking profession, in addition to teaching classroom curriculum including Hours of Service regulations.

DEDICATION

To all who have chosen the
noble profession of a
professional driver.
The hard work and dedication
to all those before, presently working,
and those yet to arrive are a
tribute to the quality of life
led by every person living in the
United States.

Table of Contents

Section One
Everything You Always Wanted to Know About the Trucking Industry

Section Two
Nine Basic Back-Up Line Illustrations

Section Three
Getting Good Directions is Critical

- Plan Your Trip in Advance, or Else
- The Other Side of the Coin
- GPS for the Tractor-Trailer
- Benefits of Having a GPS
- One Possible Disadvantage of the GPS
- Trucker's Atlas
- Calling the Consignee and Consignor
- Save Your Directions
- A Word of Caution: Low Bridges - Rotaries, Roundabouts, and Circles
- Entering and Driving Safely Around the Rotary
- Don't Depend on the CB Radio
- Asking for Help

SECTION 1

Everything You Always Wanted to Know About the Trucking Industry

The Basics
The Trucking Industry is Indispensable to the Economy

With the global economy firmly in place, seeing jobs outsourced to foreign countries, one steadfast industry that consistently remains and grows is trucking. The rail and shipping industries deliver a vast amount of freight, however, the natural logistics and economic issues that are inherent to those two modes of transportation are such that from a practical aspect, **only trucking** has the inherent flexibility to deliver product directly to the customer. The bottom line is: If the truck does not make the delivery, the store has no freight. People would not be able to shop nor purchase and, consequently, the business would have no customers.

It's important to be aware of the fact that no matter where on this earth products are manufactured, upon arrival by air or sea, the freight has to eventually be pulled by a semi-tractor-trailer. If the freight arrives by air, it will go through the proper logistics until it reaches a point of destination to be placed into a trailer. Should the freight arrive by container ship, it will most surely be stored within a container that is ready-made to be attached to a semi-tractor for delivery, TL (truck load), or LTL (less than a truck load).

The trucking industry will always be looking for professional drivers. People come and go for various reasons within the industry. The most important demand for most people is the requirement to be away from one's family for a period of time, with the general exception being that of a local driver. Additional requirements include good health and physical condition, agility, dexterity, patience, multi-tasking, and communication skills (specifically when speaking with the Safety Director, Dispatcher/Driver Manager/Fleet Manager, and the all-important customer).

The Trucking Industry Does Not Discriminate

It's a fact of life that discrimination exists within many professions, whether white-collar or blue-collar. The fact that discrimination is illegal and immoral is another subject for another time. When it comes to the trucking industry one can be confident in stating the trucking industry shines brightly when it comes to **not** discriminating. **All are welcome.**

- **Age -** Not a barrier as long as you are physically and mentally fit
- **Gender -** Male or female
- **Race/Religion -** Not an issue
- **LGBT -** How people live their personal lives, is their business

What the Trucking Industry Does Not Care About

- Formal Education Requirements - there aren't any. Although beneficial to have, a high school diploma or GED is not required. At the other educational extreme, having a bachelor's degree, master's degree, or a PhD, has no special significance regarding how well and/or how much money you will make. The "playing field" is level. It's all up to **YOU!**

What the Trucking Industry Does Care About

- People who are drug free
- People with a good driving record (every company has their own criteria)
- People who are honest
- People who are responsible
- Arriving safely with the freight
- Arriving on time with the freight

Marching to the Beat of Your Own Drummer

The trucking industry offers many benefits. One benefit that is very important to many people is the reasonably independent lifestyle. There is no boss to watch over you on a minute-by-minute basis. **As a professional driver, it is your responsibility to arrive on time and in a safe manner.**

Balancing Arriving On Time and Arriving Safely

If, for whatever reason, it is not possible to arrive on time for your "pick up" or "delivery" call your Dispatcher/Driver Manager/Fleet Manager and/or the consignee/consignor (depending on your companies' requirements). Arriving early or on time is a **very important** part of your job but it doesn't trump driving in a **safe and responsible manner.** Understanding how to properly **balance** these two critical dynamics of the trucking industry can assure a long and fruitful career.

Driving Safely is the Key

Priority #1

There is one specific criteria that **ALL** trucking companies have in common, and insist upon: **Drive Safely.** Nothing else comes close, including arriving on time.

Driving **safely** and **arriving on time** are the **two** important **"keys"** to making a productive livelihood for yourself and your family. It's that simple. **Think** as a **professional driver**.

The Purpose of this Book

To educate and enlighten every person wanting to make a living in this highly needed respectable business, the necessary information to attain the skill and back-up safely.

The backing-up of a tractor-trailer is one of the highest skill-sets any professional driver **must** master. Think about this fact: When people walk or run they normally go forward. Anytime we walk backward, either slowly or quickly, we have to think carefully about every step while also looking behind us. **Moving forward is a natural motion, while backing-up is a very unnatural motion.** Nowhere is this forward/backward juxtaposition more obvious than behind the wheel of a tractor-trailer.

The Methods Written in this Book

There is no one **"best way"** to teach the **"art of backing."** It's the most difficult element in the entire driving process to teach, learn and comprehend. The reason: Because the process is an **"art"** and the concept of any **"art form"** can be very ethereal. As with any process, the more you practice, the better you'll become, and the easier it will be to accomplish your goal(s). Mastery, however, begins with the proper learning method(s).

The methods in this book regarding this process are only one specific way to teach the **"art of backing."** No claim is being made that the methods of teaching in this book are better or worse than any other. However, having taught multitudes of people as a professional over-the-road driver and as a certified instructor, this author can attest to the fact that the methods are valid as presented and understood by the student learning the skills, **"science" _and_ "art"** of backing-up a tractor-trailer.

The Three Types of Driving

- **OTR (Over-the-Road) -** The easiest of all. New students generally ask why they may not cover hundreds and hundreds of miles during their schooling. Quite simply, as important as OTR is, it is without a doubt the easiest type of driving to learn and to perform.

- **City -** This skill level far exceeds OTR driving. Shifting and downshifting is involved, unless you are driving an automatic transmission. However, shifting and downshifting are only the beginning. There are tight corners to go around, narrow streets, winding roads, cars darting out of driveways, cars darting around the tractor-trailer because they have no patience, traffic lights with a timing sequence that has been designed for cars, etc. The list could extend almost indefinitely. However, when it comes to making money based on miles, the money is in OTR driving.

- **Backing-Up -** Backing-Up successfully requires a very high skill level that requires time and patience. Many people already in the industry, and most certainly new drivers, find backing-up a tractor-trailer the most difficult skill to acquire. **Backing-Up is as unnatural to driving as it is to walking backward.** Yet, it **most certainly** can be accomplished in a **safe and effective manner** if you truly **understand** the criteria and concepts required. **They are not difficult. They just take time to grasp.**

The Elements of Backing-Up

Backing-Up is a Science

It's **important** to **first understand** the basic **"science of backing"** prior to discussing or performing the **"art of backing."** The **science** as too how a tractor and trailer function is **cut and dry,** however the **art** of understanding how to manipulate and maneuver both vehicles **definitely is not.**

When backing-up an automobile, the process is straight forward. Whichever way the steering wheel is turned (left or right), the back end of the vehicle will **ALWAYS** move in that same direction.

When backing-up a tractor-trailer the process is different. The fifth wheel connection to the trailer will make the **front of the trailer *pivot*** toward the same side that the steering wheel has been turned, thereby causing the **back-end of the trailer** to *angle* towards the **opposite** side. It's basically a chain reaction**. Refer to Section Two titled: "Nine Basic Line Illustrations."**

When you are performing a straight-line back-up, the objective of keeping the alignment perfectly straight is the same as all other configurations required to back-up. Whichever direction you want the back of the trailer to move toward (left or right), you **MUST** turn the steering wheel in the **OPPOSITE DIRECTION**.

IT'S IMPORTANT TO UNDERSTAND THE SCIENCE OF BACKING-UP A TRACTOR-TRAILER BEFORE TRYING TO ATTEMPT THE PROCESS

IT IS EASIER THAN IT SEEMS, IF THE SCIENCE IS UNDERSTOOD FIRST

- When backing-up a tractor-trailer, the **BACK-END** of the trailer will move in the **OPPOSITE** direction of the way you are turning the steering wheel.
- EXAMPLE: When you turn the steering wheel to the **LEFT**, the back-end of the trailer will move to the **RIGHT** (and vice versa).

Backing-Up is an Art and a Process

The *art* of backing-up a tractor-trailer must be thought of in a totally different way from the *science.* The *science* of backing-up a tractor-trailer is **"cut and dry."** Whereas understanding the *art* of how to properly and safely back-up a tractor-trailer can be baffling, subtle, puzzling, unspecific, and elusive. There are multiple things to look at and watch for simultaneously. Get the **"BIG PICTURE,"** be **detail oriented** and **drive defensively. Think** and **"feel"** the flow of moving the tractor and trailer properly and safely toward its destination.

Setting-Up the Tractor and Trailer

With all thing being equal: The difference between struggling and not struggling when backing-up is the **understanding of how to implement a proper set-up.** Every situation is unique and requires skill, ability, and experience to cover every possible scenario you will encounter. Learn the basics through every means possible. Doing so will inevitably develop your skills and enable you to back-up with a high degree of confidence, backing safely into the countless number of places that are critical to being a professional truck driver.

LTD (Look - Think - Drive)

The process of driving forward or backward share one consistent rule:

- **Look -** Always look and observe the area in which you are preparing to move toward.
- **Think -** What you will have to contend with and how you are going to achieve your goal.
- **Drive -** Knowing as much information in advance, while consistently looking and thinking, are a key to arriving at your destination safely.

Just a Piece of Metal

The tractor and trailer are mechanical devices that have no thoughts or feelings. They will go toward whichever direction you tell them, forward or backward. **You** are the one in total control, and the key to control is: Knowing **how** and **when** to turn the steering wheel.

Questions and Answers About Backing-Up a Tractor-Trailer

Q. What is the first step to begin the process of backing-up a tractor-trailer?

A. <u>RELAX!</u> This one key factor is essential to the success of being a professional driver regardless of whatever has to be accomplished at any given time. Maintaining a calm demeanor, as it relates to backing-up, is paramount to being able to accomplish your goal of backing-up safely. **Relaxation is the first step** before you ever proceed to safely back-up.

Q. What is the second step?

A. Turn off the radio and never feel intimidated by any person or persons watching you. **Refer to Section One titled: "Never Allow Yourself to Become Intimated."**

Q. What is the third step?

A. Create the best possible set-up. Knowing how too properly set-up a tractor-trailer is based on the physical space you have available. It's a skill to be learned! **Think as a professional.** The **proper set-up** will determine how **easy** or **difficult** your back-up will be. View the entire area **horizontally** and **vertically** while also looking out for any other obstructions such as poles, high wires, overhangs, cars, people traffic, etc. **Think about the height, width, and length of the tractor and trailer**. You are **pushing** the trailer toward the location where it needs to be as you are moving backward. **The better your set-up is, the easier your back-up will be.**

Q. Is there anything I should do, after observing the area I need to back into, that can make the process safer before backing-up?

A. (1) **Engage the Flashers!** Alert everyone around you whether, they are a pedestrian or a driver in a vehicle, as to your presence. **Always** leave the flashers on until the back-up is complete.

 (2) **Use an existing (and/or set-up your own) point or points of reference.** This can be almost anything you could think of. Examples might include a tree, a curb, a car, a building, etc. The list is infinite. If a natural point of reference does **not** exist, then **create**

your own. Example: Place your own reference point(s), such as a piece of metal or some other indestructible object approximately ¼" in height and at least 12" square or round. The object(s) being used **must** be very bright in color so it can be seen from the driver's viewpoint during the entire process. The small height of the reference point(s) will not cause any damage to the tires, and the large width can be seen more easily. Every professional driver should create their own "reference point" object(s) and carry them on every trip.

The number of reference points needed, are up to each driver. Only one may be necessary, or possibly three or four could work better. It's a personal decision based on your comfort zone, *and* your needs, in order to back-up safely. Every back-up stands on its own merits. The rule is: There is no rule for the amount of reference points you may need, or choose to create, in order to maintain a safe back-up. **Refer to Section Two: It contains various illustrations demonstrating placed reference points.**

Q. If I have an option to back into an available space that does not have any vehicles on either side, regardless of where I am (rest area, truck stop, delivery point, etc.) can I, or should I, back-in?

A. (1) **Absolutely!** Anytime you have an opportunity to back into a space that has nothing on the left or right side of your objective parking destination, **take it.**

(2) If you have the specific option to back into a space that has no vehicles or objects on your right side (blind side), **take it.**

Q. Does the position of the tandems have an effect in backing-up the tractor and trailer?

A. **Yes.** However it depends on the space available. The further you slide the tandems forward, the greater will be the overhang of the rear portion of the trailer. It's important to remember that even when you perform a sight-side back-up, until the tractor and trailer are perfectly aligned with each other, the **right side** is, and must **always** be, considered the **blind-side.**

- Remain constantly aware of the overhang. It can be deceiving. The further the tandems are placed toward the rear of the trailer, the safer it is to back-up especially when any vehicle or object is on your blind side.

- When the space to back into is **tight,** or especially **very tight,** it may be the appropriate time to slide the tandems more forward toward the front before proceeding. Doing this will allow the pivot to angle quicker, and place the trailer into the **limited space** you have to work with. When doing this, always be aware of the **added overhang** of the trailer as you are backing-up. Any time you are ever in doubt and the back-up you are attempting is dubious, there is only one thing to do: **GOAL (Get out and look). Refer to Section One titled: "GOAL (Get Out and Look)."**

Q. At what speed is it best to back-up the tractor and trailer?

A. Back-Up <u>V - E - R - Y</u>   <u>S - L - O - W - L - Y</u>! **Refer to Section One titled: "It's About Liability - Speed: The Slower, the Better."**

Q. When backing-up, a tractor-trailer, is the steering wheel turned the same way I would turn to back-up a car?

A. NO! The steering wheel <u>**cannot**</u> be turned the same way as a car. The average car is one structure that is approximately 12-14 feet long, whereas a tractor-trailer may be approximately 75 feet long depending on factors such as day cab, sleeper cab, and the length of the trailer. The concept and process to back-up a car is **completely different** as compared to a tractor-trailer.

- **Important:** The shorter the trailer, the quicker it will turn.

Q. How much should the steering wheel be turned as I back-up?

A. There is no specific answer. Every situation is different depending on the **length *and* width** of the available space you are backing into. Experience will enable you to determine how much you need to turn from the beginning to the end of the maneuver. One **important** factor regarding the art of backing-up a tractor-trailer is to **turn the steering wheel quickly.** This is also referred to as **turning the steering wheel hard**. They essentially mean the same thing. If the steering wheel is turned too slowly, the trailer will be ahead of you, as to where you want it to go, due to the **"delay reaction"** instead of you being ahead of the trailer.

Q. Explain the "delay reaction" when the wheel is turned?

A. Depending on the tractor being a day cab (that generally has a single axle), versus a sleeper cab (that most certainly will have a twin axle) the time sequence from one point to another will vary. A shorter trailer will affect a varied delay as well. **Anticipate** the **"delay reaction"** and turn the wheel **accordingly** and **quickly.** The delay can vary between approximately four to eight feet before the tandems turn in the direction you want them to.

Q. I only have to turn the wheel ¼ of a turn as the trailer is moving backward. Should I still turn it quickly?

A. Yes! It may seem abnormal, however, turning the wheel **quickly regardless of how much it needs to be turned,** will place the trailer where it needs to be sooner. That fact is an important part of the process developed with experience. This is because of the **"delay reaction."**

Q. Is there a reaction difference when turning the steering wheel in a single axle vs. a twin axle tractor?

A. Absolutely. As important as it is to turn the steering wheel quickly when you drive a single axle tractor, the steering wheel must be turned even sooner and quicker to compensate for the tractor that has twin axles. Again, this is because of the **"delay reaction."**

Q. What is the right way to counter-steer?

A. The process is exactly the same as steering the tractor and trailer. Turn the steering wheel **quickly** and **watch** the appropriate mirrors. **Constantly** know the position of the tractor, while always following the trailer and tandems.

Q. When I back-up I seem to jack-knife a lot. Why?

A. Jack-knifing is almost always due to **NOT** anticipating the **"delay reaction"** that will inevitably take place during the process of backing-up. **Think** and **stay ahead** of the trailer throughout the entire time you are backing-up. Turning the steering wheel **quickly** throughout the process will help you **immensely** toward your goal. This important factor is one of many others necessary to know that is unique and separates a Class A license from all others, as well as numerous regulations.

Q. How much and how soon should the mirrors be watched?

A. Always watch **all** appropriate mirrors **as much** and **as soon** as is needed to back-up safely. During the process of backing-up a tractor-trailer, you may find yourself turning your head back and forth any number of times. Five times, ten times, twenty times, fifty times; whatever is required to back-up safely is the key to success.

Q. How can the trailer be followed when there is no rear window?

A. Regardless of whether or not the tractor is a day cab that probably has a rear window, or a sleeper cab that does not, **always** be using your mirrors, both west coast and convex, in addition to looking out the front and side windows when appropriate. **Knowing when and how to use the windows and mirrors is a prime key to backing safely. Never lose sight of where the tractor, trailer, and tandems are located, relative to the available space.**

Q. How do I know if the trailer is moving in the right direction?

A. Follow the **rear** of the trailer and the **tandems.** It's **critical** to understand this concept. Too repeat: The process of backing-up a tractor-trailer has **no resemblance** to how a car is backed-up. **Think as a professional driver, and forget completely about your car.**

Q. How do I know when to make a correction?

A. Follow the path you visualize and want to follow, always watching the trailer and tandems. When you can see you are not on track, **immediately** make the appropriate correction. **Stay ahead** by **anticipating** the **"delay reaction."**

- Making quick, short, easy corrections is the key.
- The longer you take to make the correction, the greater the correction will be.

Q. At what point should I begin turning the steering wheel when the space available is limited?

A. Turn the steering wheel **before** you move back even **one inch.** Knowing how much to turn is an educated guess. Driving a single axle tractor will change the timing for turning the steering wheel as compared to a twin axle tractor. Turning the steering wheel **before** moving can make the backing process a lot easier and less stressful. Anytime the amount of space is tighter and more limiting to work with, the **"delay reaction,"** along with the length of tractor and trailer, can make it difficult to achieve your goal if you do not compensate for the minimal space that is available.

- If you make a mistake by turning the wheel in the wrong direction, especially if the space available is tight, you may have lost the footage you need in order to place the trailer into the desired space. **If this happens, don't struggle. Pull-Up.**

Note: The steering wheel can be turned immediately even if the space available is not tight. There is no specific formula. **Backing-Up is an art form.** You are plotting out and painting the proper course on the ground **"in your mind."**

Q. How do I know when and how I should perform a pull-up?

A. This question is so **important**, it has been written about in a section. **Refer to Section One titled: "The Point of No Return: Pull-Up, Pull-Up, Pull-Up."**

Q. If I am not positive regarding the requirements needed to back-up accident free, what should I do?

A. GOAL (Get Out and Look). Refer to Section One titled: "GOAL (Get out and Look)."

Q. As I am watching the trailer when backing-up, at what point do I watch the tractor?

A. At the **same time** (especially when the space is tight). Multitasking is **very important!** A professional driver can never have tunnel vision. **Multitask constantly,** and that includes going forward as well. The ability and use of multitasking will serve you well.

- Use your peripheral vision
- Move your eyes
- Move your head
- Watch the mirrors constantly

Q. Is it a good idea to use a spotter?

A. Maybe! Maybe not! If you don't know who the person is, there are basic questions you must find an answer for before you can make this decision.

1. Does this person **appear** to understand the process of backing-up?

2. Do you **think** you can **trust** the person who is spotting for you?

The decision to **use** or **not use** a person to help guide you rests completely on your shoulders. Be certain to make the call with much thought about the consequences. If your decision was a bad one, and an accident was caused because **incorrect information** was given to you, **keep in mind,** the **legality** rests upon the **person driving, regardless** of any other person giving directions.

Q. What if the person spotting for me is my "team driver"?

A. Maybe! Maybe not! At least you know this person, which definitely helps to alleviate that **"sense of trust."** However, there are still basic questions that you need answered in your own mind. The answer **may rest** with **how well** and, **what you know** about the person you are team driving with.

(1) **Person #1 - New driver (No relation):** A greater risk considering their skill level is not that experienced.

(2) **Person #2 - Experienced driver (No relation):** Obviously a better scenario. Remember: You are still the person responsible in the event of an accident.

(3) **Person #3 - Husband/Wife team/Relative:** Best scenario. At least you know who this person is; however there is still a question to be answered. Does this person have the knowledge and experience backing-up a tractor-trailer. **Do not forget: The driver of the vehicle is the person responsible. Period!**

Q. I have no choice but to perform a blind-side back-up due to the space, location, one-way street, etc. What is the best way to safely back-up?

A. Blind-side backing is the exact opposite of sight-side backing, but, because the blind-side is not the "natural side" it can be **considerably** more confusing. Some trucking companies have created a policy of letting drivers know there is no tolerance allowable for blind-side backing. It's important to know the policy of your company's Safety Director. If blind-side backing is allowable, and you have no choice, there are some general procedures you can follow:

- Use a trusted spotter. With the trusted spotter generally situated standing in front of the tractor, continually walking back and forth from the blind-side to the sight-side, you can be properly guided into the space up to the point you will not need the assistance.

- Should you have no choice but to back-up with no help, you must back-up being overly cautious.
- Use the motorized mirror(s) constantly (if you have one on the passenger side)
- Back up **S-L-O-W-L-Y "inch-by-inch,"** and **"foot by foot."**
- **GOAL (Get Out and Look)** as much as you think is necessary to back-up safely.
- Take all the time you need! Never be intimidated or concerned you may be holding up traffic, cars, etc. Read more on this subject in Section 1 titled: **Never Allow Yourself to Become Intimidated.**
- Eventually, with the correct process, your tractor will swing to the sight-side and you can complete the procedure as a sight-side back-up.
- The **key** to blind-side *and* sight-side backing is: **Never Lose Your Patience!**

Q. Why is it that almost every time I back into a space, (even if it's the same space multiple times, on the same day or not), each back-up requires its own unique maneuvers?

A. Backing-Up is an art. Don't waste your time trying to duplicate yourself. Never expect to duplicate the exact same backing maneuver. The objective is to back-up safely. Every back-up is unique and different. Every back-up requires a new and different set-up depending on the surrounding conditions. The prime concern is always **SAFETY.**

Q. Is there any other method I can use to learn the process of backing-up a tractor-trailer safely?

A. YES! In addition to the information you have learned from reading this book, you can speak to professional truck drivers, and **WATCH** them back-up their vehicles. Take the time to go to a truck stop and watch the process taking place. Look at their "body language." How and when they move their head back and forth to view the appropriate mirror, or rolling down driver's or passengers window to get a better view, are just some of the pointers that can be learned by observation.

In addition to watching a professional driver, take the time to walk over and speak to someone. There are many people out there who are more than willing to share valuable information that can be of immense help to you.

Drive Safely

Arrive Safely

Back-Up Safely

It's About Liability
Speed: The Slower, The Better

Never Rush the Process

Given the knowledge, skill, and patience required to back-up a tractor-trailer, it is **imperative** to **always** think and function as a professional driver. All levels of management, from the owner(s) of the trucking company flowing to every other department within the organization, require first and foremost that **safety is paramount** in order for the company to thrive. The requirements of **safety** and **understanding liability** must flow directly to every professional driver as well.

Without the element of safety being the highest priority, there is no trucking company that can exist in the marketplace. The basic facts are:

* **The DOT (Department of Transportation)** could shut the company down, or fine them out of existence, due to consistent safety issues.
* **The insurance industry** has safety at the very top on its priority list as to which trucking companies they will insure and for what cost. Any trucking company with a poor safety record (that is able to find liability insurance) will ultimately be forced to pay substantially higher premiums, thereby making them less competitive in the market place.
* **As a professional driver,** your self-interest is to work for a quality trucking company that can provide:
* 1. Steady employment at a competitive pay rate.
* 2. Health, pension, and safety bonus benefits.
* 3. Security: This is one business that cannot be outsourced, but the trucking company must be financially viable in order to provide the viable employment you are looking for. Safety **must** remain the prime factor above all other aspects of the industry. The DOT and the insurance companies will **always** keep safety as their prime concern and responsibility. That mindset **must** flow to all trucking companies, and professional drivers in order to have the entire trucking industry and the economy thrive.
* As a professional driver, it is your responsibility to think **safety *and* liability at all times,** driving **forward *and* backing-up.**

- Due to the complexity of the backing process, anytime you back-up, always back **slowly.** Should **slowly** be too fast for your given situation, then back **very slowly,** and if that seems to be too fast then simply **crawl** backward into your space. Another few minutes of time spent backing-up safely is negligible to however long you may find yourself spending taking pictures, writing up an accident report, speaking with a police officer, and calling your Safety Director.
- Always have a camera in your possession. Your camera can be **"your best friend"** at the moment you need it. **Protect your interests.**

Never Allow Yourself to Become Intimidated

Rule #1

Never allow yourself to become intimidated because other people are watching you back-up. It can be a very disconcerting, detrimental factor that will reflect negatively on the concentration required to back-up safely. Intimidation can be one of the causes for accidents that should **never happen** to anyone who is in control of his or her emotions.

Dock Workers - Truck Drivers - Gawkers

Arriving at a location (whether it's at a truck stop, rest area, or a delivery location) that requires a slow, methodical, time-consuming back-up in order to be safe, will at times attract an **"audience."**

- **Dock Workers:** When people working at a dock may not be busy, for whatever reason, your arrival provides them **"entertainment."** Should you notice one or more congregating upon your arrival, keep your emotions in check, ignore your **"audience,"** and proceed as the professional driver you know you are.

- Should the dock space be tight, or possibly have tractor-trailers already docked to the immediate left and right of your space, you may begin to notice people gathering at the dock to see if you have the **"right stuff"** required to back-up safely. The **"show"** has just started. Don't even be surprised if you notice money being passed around. It's no secret that dock workers who consistently view tractor-trailers coming and going will place a bet on whether or not you can back into your space without creating an accident.

- **Truck Drivers:** Other drivers who just happen to be in the area for whatever reason, and are interested in seeing just how professional a driver you really are. Many **will help you** should the need arise. One **"very interested"** driver could be the one who is already parked to the immediate left and/or right of your space, watching with intense interest to see if you are going to cause an accident by backing into their tractor or trailer.

- **Note:** If you are having difficulty, this may very well be the time to ask for help from one of the drivers in the area. Don't be surprised if another driver actually volunteers to guide you back. He or she may be the driver of the vehicle to the immediate right or left of your space, or maybe not. That person may just be a driver in the area who sees you having issues and wants to genuinely help. Keep in mind **you** are the **responsible party regardless** of who the person(s) is helping to guide you back.
- **Gawkers:** People who have nothing else to do at the moment. Construction workers refer to them as **"sidewalk superintendents."**
- As a professional driver, expect to experience all three of the above, and more. Just perform in the way and manner you know is correct, and amazingly you will see people just quietly walk away. The **"show"** is over in their mind, and it's on to the next event in their lives.

It's Time to Back-Up

- Use an existing, *or* place your own point(s) of reference, if necessary.
- **Note:** Should you be driving a manual transmission, be certain your vehicle is in low range.
- **Set-Up the tractor and trailer properly.**
- Roll down the driver's side window and the passenger side window if you need a clearer view of all the space around and behind you, especially when it is more difficult to discern **EXACTLY** what is on your right side. Rain and diminished natural or artificial light are prime reasons to roll down either window. It will most assuredly be the passenger side that can cause a problem, as your eyes are viewing four to five feet across the cab, and through a piece of glass, into a mirror. Night-time backing definitely requires extra vigilance. **ALWAYS** keep your mirrors and windows clean.
- **Go back very slowly, foot-by-foot.** Be methodical. **Ignore** any **"audience"** around you.
- **Anticipate** the **"delay reaction"** (even more-so when the space is tight).
- **When you consider it necessary, especially when the space is tight:** You can control the tractor and trailer safely by using the method of **"turning and stopping"** as needed. Every time you do **stop,** it allows you to **think** about the proper way to proceed.
- Follow your path. **Draw a "line" in your mind** as to the **track** you want the **trailer** and **tandems** to move toward.
- **Always** be aware of how much **trailer overhang** there is, referenced to the location of the rear tandems.

- **Be aware of your blind side.** The space on your right side is either **occupied *or* vacant** of other vehicles and/or objects, people, low overhangs, etc. Knowing all this and retaining the information as you back-up is important.

- **GOAL (Get Out and Look). Pull-up as many times as you think you need.** Just make certain that each action **improves your situation.**

- Once you get to the point of **seeing *and* knowing** your maneuvers are complete, it may very well be the appropriate time to straighten out the tractor aligning it to the trailer. You will **easily** be able to view **both sides** of your vehicle and the trailer via your mirrors. Should you think one more **GOAL (Get Out and Look), is prudent, do it.** The rest should be a cake-walk.

The Point of No Return: Pull-Up, Pull-Up, Pull-Up

Correct Your Situation

Whenever you **"think"** *and* **"know"** as a professional driver you have reached the inevitable point when it makes no sense whatsoever to continue to keep going backwards as you are approaching your docking space, the only sensible, logical, proper thing to do is **pull-up.**

The purpose for pulling-up your tractor-trailer is about **"improving your situation,"** by **"resetting the vehicles,"** thereby **"fixing the problem."** The method of utilizing one or more pull-ups is what professional drivers have always done in order to properly back-up and maintain a safe driving record.

How Many Pull-Ups?

There is no answer to this question as long as you, as a professional, know what is required to back-up safely. Some pull-ups may require you to drive your tractor-trailer forward all the way to the beginning of your set-up, or possibly only a short distance forward may be necessary. The combined location of the tractor, trailer, and placement of the tandems **as they all relate to the dock space** is what you need to evaluate.

When Pulling-Up, Pull-Up Properly

- **Relax, think,** *and* **survey** the area you are dealing with.
- Before you proceed to pull-up, think about how you want to **set-up** your vehicles. This will depend on all the elements around and within the space you have available.

    (1) **Straight Line:** Pull-Up placing the tractor to the trailer in perfect alignment to each other.

    (2) **Alley Dock:** Pull-Up placing the tractor to the trailer facing toward the left side of the trailer, generally at a 45 degree angle (11:00 o'clock).

    (3) **Don't leave yourself blindsided** because you placed the tractor to the right side of the trailer. There can be an exception to this however, it would be **extremely rare.**

22

(4) **Pull-Up as far as it is necessary.** (When your tractor, trailer and tandems are in the proper position to accomplish your goal, there is generally no need to pull-up any further).

• Pulling-Up properly will allow you to see the rear of the trailer, the tandems, and the dock space considerably easier.

GOAL (Get Out and Look)

The Importance of GOAL

GOAL is the most important acronym in the professional driver's "book of knowledge." There are never enough words to emphatically state the importance of **"getting out of your vehicle and looking." Survey the entire area before you proceed.** Complete this one **critical** step **anytime** you are **not positive** the situation **all around** you is safe to back-up.

> **AS A PROFESSIONAL DRIVER, REPEATING THIS ONE PROCEDURE AS MANY TIMES AS NECESSARY IS A KEY FACTOR TOWARD LONGEVITY IN THE BUSINESS.**

The Intimidation Factor

Many a driver (especially those new to the business) will allow themselves to become intimidated because other people in the vicinity may possibly be watching the **"show"** of the big rig backing-up.

You are **not** in a Broadway show, but your **"audience"** around who is viewing you backing-up sees it as a **"performance."** Be professional. **Get Out and Look** when you know it is the right thing to do in order to back-up **safely.**

Arriving at Your Destination

Stop and Assess the Situation

This is especially important if this is your first time arriving to pick up or drop off freight. There are numerous considerations that can create difficulty if you do not assess the conditions properly.

Examples of what You May Encounter

- **Situation:** You are stopped at a red light that is directly across the street from the location you need to enter.

- **Solution:** Scan the area for the proper entrance, signs, etc. The sign may or may not be legible or easy to read, or the weather may be inclement. Take your time when you are not certain as to what you need to do.

Note: There may be a sign that states "Truck Entrance Left Side of Building," or "All Trucks Go Around to Back of Building." The point is there are literally hundreds of expressions you will encounter on handwritten and professionally designed signs. Some will state "Cars Only" or "Truck Entrance Only."

- **Situation:** The entrance is down the street on the right side. Caution: If you drive too close to the entrance, you may have to back-up, because you will not have enough horizontal space for the **"swing"** of the trailer.

- **Solution:** Get the **"Big Picture"** and, if necessary, slow down and stop. **Use the flashers.** This can allow you the time to make the correct decision and safely move toward your left, thereby giving you the room to enter.

- **Situation:** Driving on a street toward your destination, you spot the entrance. You are not certain, and/or you don't like your **"set-up"** at the time.

- **Solution:** Continue to drive until you can pull over safely. Walk to or call the customer. Put on your flashers.

- **Situation:** As you arrive, you are not quite sure what to do, however, you notice a nearby vacant parking lot large enough for your tractor and trailer nearby.

- <u>**Solution:**</u> Drive into the parking lot. What a relief! This will give you the time to access the area, and/or possibly get out (shut off the engine, take the keys, and lock the doors). Speak to the person(s) at your arrival point for the information you need.

The list of possible circumstances is almost endless. With each point of arrival every situation will warrant its own specific solutions. The more information you can have in advance, the better off, easier and safer your arrival will be. Refer to Section Three titled: "Getting Good Directions is Critical."

C S A
Compliance - Safety - Accountability

Know the Federal Laws

The age-old phrase **"knowledge is power"** is especially relevant when it comes to having a basic knowledge of the federal law that maintains records on every DOT registered trucking company in the United States.

The Safety Measurement System (SMS) provides an extensive profile of all commercial motor carriers and drivers, relative to interstate and intrastate driving. The laws are inclusive relative to companies that carry cargo as well as passengers, hazmat, and non-hazmat.

The implementation and concepts of the law have been designed to improve large truck and bus safety compliance to prevent future crashes, injuries, and fatalities, and ultimately make all the roads throughout the entire country safer for everyone.

- A multitude of basic DOT criteria for assessing a scoring system, that includes public access information on commercial trucking companies, can be found on the following website: **http://ai.fmcsa.dot.gov/sms/**
- Input any company registered with the DOT by inputting their DOT number at the above listed website. Search for Motor Carrier SMS Monthly Results, and the public access information will upload.

The Basic Categories of CSA
Public Access

- Unsafe driving
- Hours-of-Service (HOS) Compliance
- Driver Fitness
- Controlled Substances and Alcohol
- Vehicle Maintenance

Non-Public Access

- Hazmat Compliance
- Crash Indicator

    1. Lists of Crashes

    2. Roadside Inspections

    3. Violations from Roadside Inspections

    4. Driver names and other privacy related material from individual inspection results.

SECTION TWO

Nine Basic Back-Up Line Illustrations

Important Information

This section contains illustrations that complement the basic back-up situations encountered when driving a tractor-trailer. Each backing-up scenario (of which there are literally hundreds) has its own specific elements all professional drivers must be constantly aware of, and understand how to overcome, in order to make it realistically viable to **back-up safely.**

There will be times when backing-up into a location may be quite literally **impossible** due to **circumstances beyond your control.** Perhaps an automobile has been parked in an area that it should not be in, or maybe the horizontal space on the left or right side of the dock location presents a critical problem to your being able to safely back into.

Each and every situation **must** stand on its own merits in regards to having a realistic amount of space required for a safe **back-up.** Make a calculated professional decision with **EVERY** back-up. When it's **NOT** possible - **DO NOT** attempt to back-up. Speak to a person who has the **authority** to correct the problem.

LEARNING THE FUNDAMENTAL CONCEPT OF HOW A TRACTOR AND TRAILER OPERATE AS *"ONE"* VEHICLE IS THE <u>FIRST</u> <u>STEP</u> TOO UNDERSTANDING THE <u>*"ART"*</u> OF <u>BACKING-UP.</u>

THE MECHANICS OF TURNING THE STEERING WHEEL WHILE BACKING-UP

THE MECHANICS OF
TURNING THE STEERING WHEEL
WHILE BACKING-UP

**TURN THE WHEEL LEFT
TRAILER WILL MOVE RIGHT**

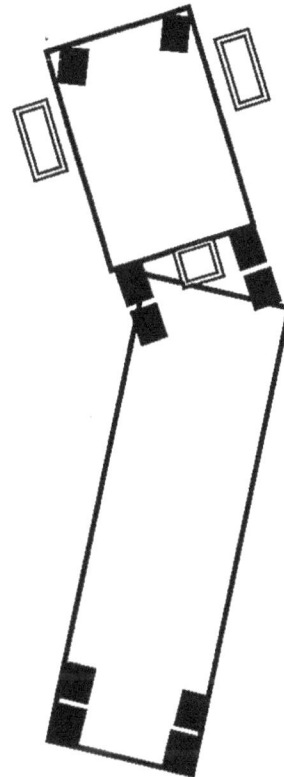

**TURN THE WHEEL RIGHT
TRAILER WILL MOVE LEFT**

ALL OF THE ABOVE STATEMENTS ARE WRITTEN IN STONE

**THE PROCESS OF BACKING A
TRACTOR-TRAILER IS A LEARNED ART**

**THE TRACTOR IS ONE VEHICLE, AND THE TRAILER IS ANOTHER.
BOTH ARE CONNECTED TO THE 5TH WHEEL THAT ALLOWS THE
TRAILER TO PIVOT FROM LEFT TO RIGHT. IT'S THAT PROCESS
THAT IS THE ART OF BACKING.**

31

SIGHT-SIDE
ALLEY DOCK
WITH TANDEMS SLID BACK

THE TANDEMS AND THE BACK-END OF THE
TRAILER ARE CLOSE TO EACH OTHER.

FOLLOW THE PATH OF THE REAR TANDEMS,
AND THE BACK-END OF THE TRAILER
VERTICALLY AND HORIZONTALLY.

* ANTICIPATE THE "DELAY REACTION" *

* USE REFERENCE POINTS *

CONSTANTLY VIEW THE LEFT AND RIGHT
MIRRORS AS NEEDED.

TURN THE STEERING WHEEL QUICKLY, ALWAYS
FOLLOWING THE PATH OF THE REAR TANDEMS,
AND THE BACK-END OF THE TRAILER.

WHEN THE SPACE IS TIGHT, TURN
THE STEERING WHEEL BEFORE PULLING-UP.

SIGHT-SIDE ALLEY DOCK
WITH TANDEMS SLID BACK

POINTS OF REFERENCE
WHEN THE CONDITIONS WARRANT, CREATE YOUR OWN POINTS OF REFERENCE

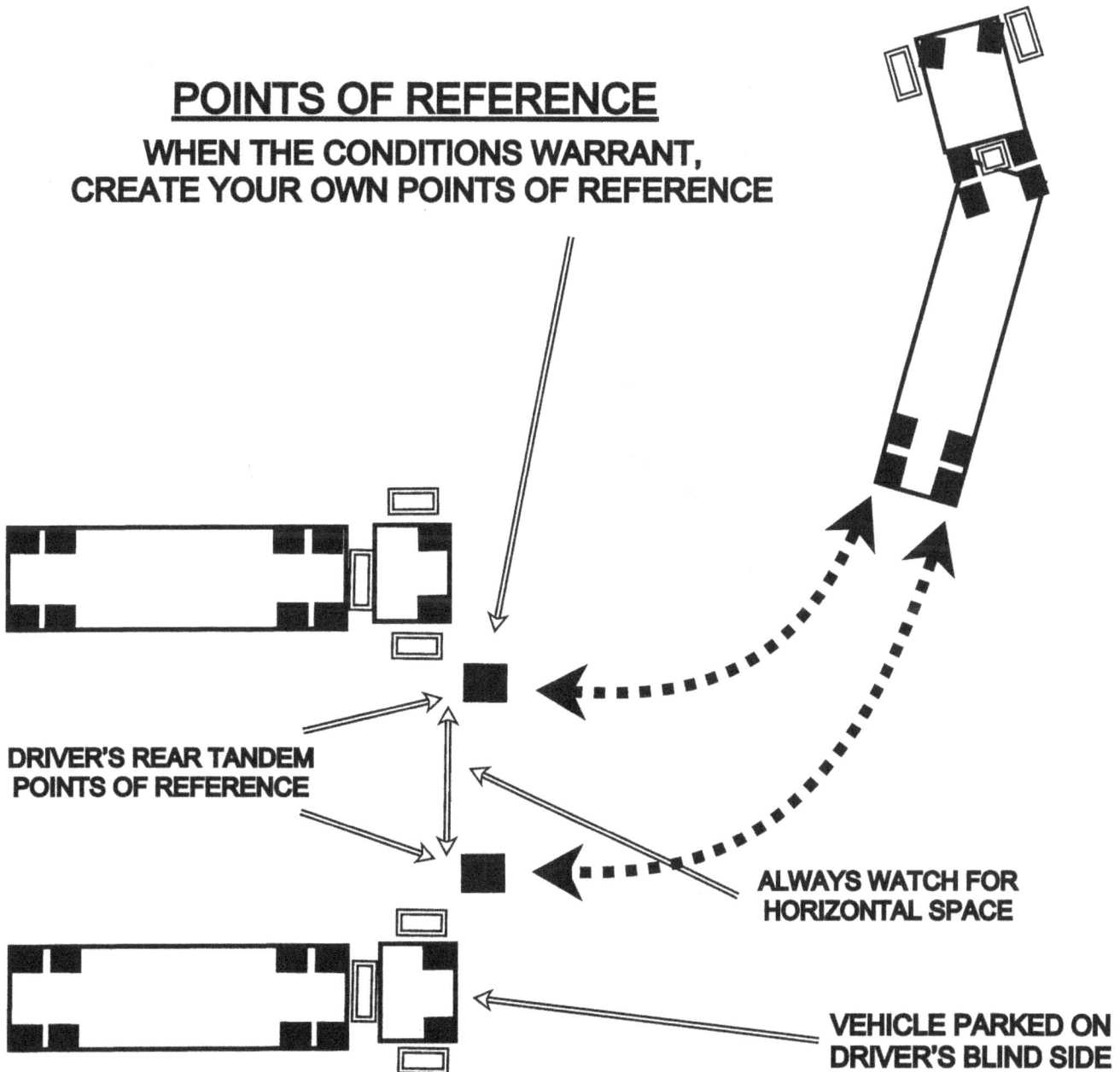

DRIVER'S REAR TANDEM POINTS OF REFERENCE

ALWAYS WATCH FOR HORIZONTAL SPACE

VEHICLE PARKED ON DRIVER'S BLIND SIDE

ADDITIONAL CAUTION MUST BE TAKEN DUE TO VEHICLE PARKED ON DRIVER'S BLIND SIDE

SIGHT-SIDE ALLEY DOCK
WITH TANDEMS SLID FORWARD

THE TANDEMS AND THE BACK-END OF THE TRAILER ARE NOT CLOSE TO EACH OTHER.

FOLLOW THE PATH OF THE REAR TANDEMS, AND THE BACK-END OF THE TRAILER VERTICALLY AND HORIZONTALLY.

* ANTICIPATE THE "DELAY REACTION" *

* USE REFERENCE POINTS *

BE AWARE OF THE TRAILER OVERHANG

CONSTANTLY VIEW THE LEFT AND RIGHT MIRRORS AS NEEDED.

TURN THE STEERING WHEEL QUICKLY, ALWAYS FOLLOWING THE PATH OF THE REAR TANDEMS, AND THE BACK-END OF THE TRAILER.

WHEN THE SPACE IS TIGHT, TURN THE STEERING WHEEL BEFORE PULLING-UP.

SIGHT-SIDE ALLEY DOCK
WITH TANDEMS SLID FORWARD

POINTS OF REFERENCE

WHEN THE CONDITIONS WARRANT,
CREATE YOUR OWN POINTS OF REFERENCE

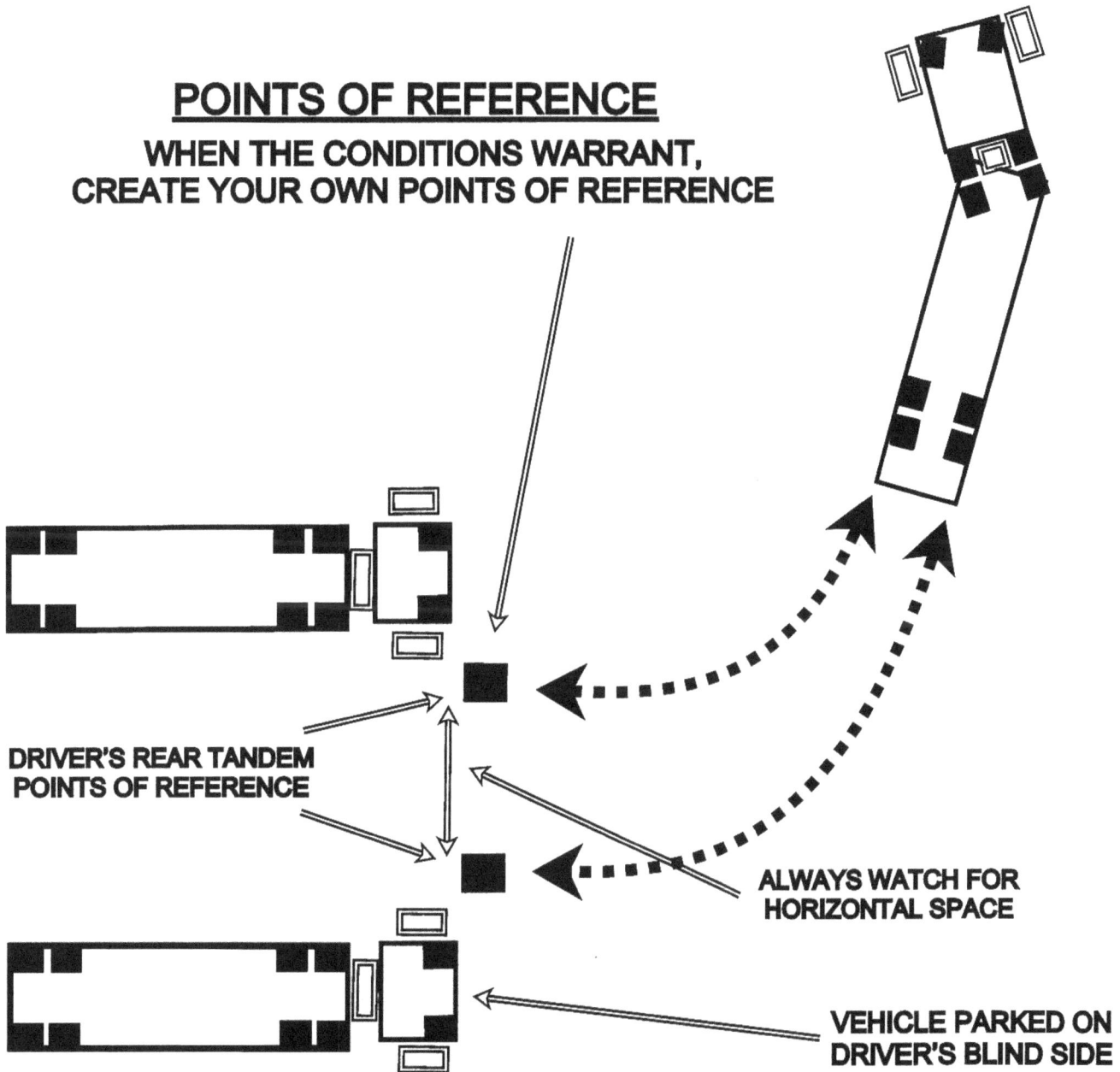

**DRIVER'S REAR TANDEM
POINTS OF REFERENCE**

**ALWAYS WATCH FOR
HORIZONTAL SPACE**

**VEHICLE PARKED ON
DRIVER'S BLIND SIDE**

ADDITIONAL CAUTION MUST BE TAKEN DUE TO
VEHICLE PARKED ON DRIVER'S BLIND SIDE

BLIND-SIDE ALLEY DOCK
WITH TANDEMS SLID BACK

THE <u>TANDEMS</u> AND THE <u>BACK-END</u> OF THE <u>TRAILER</u> <u>ARE</u> <u>CLOSE</u> TO <u>EACH</u> <u>OTHER.</u>

<u>FOLLOW</u> THE <u>PATH</u> OF THE <u>REAR</u> <u>TANDEMS,</u> AND THE <u>BACK-END</u> OF THE <u>TRAILER</u> <u>VERTICALLY</u> AND <u>HORIZONTALLY.</u>

* <u>ANTICIPATE</u> <u>THE</u> "<u>DELAY</u> <u>REACTION</u>" *

* <u>USE</u> <u>REFERENCE</u> <u>POINTS</u> *

<u>CONSTANTLY</u> <u>VIEW</u> THE <u>LEFT</u> AND <u>RIGHT</u> <u>MIRRORS</u> AS <u>NEEDED.</u>

<u>TURN</u> THE <u>STEERING</u> <u>WHEEL</u> <u>QUICKLY,</u> <u>ALWAYS</u> <u>FOLLOWING</u> THE <u>PATH</u> OF THE <u>REAR</u> <u>TANDEMS,</u> AND THE <u>BACK-END</u> OF THE <u>TRAILER.</u>

<u>REGARDLESS</u> OF THE <u>POSITION</u> OF THE <u>TANDEMS,</u> <u>EXTREME</u> <u>CAUTION</u> <u>MUST</u> BE TAKEN, SHOULD IT BE <u>NECESSARY</u> TO <u>CONDUCT</u> THIS <u>PROCEDURE.</u>

WHEN THE SPACE IS <u>TIGHT,</u> TURN THE STEERING WHEEL <u>BEFORE</u> PULLING-UP.

BLIND-SIDE ALLEY DOCK
WITH TANDEMS SLID BACK

BEING BLIND-SIDED MEANS THE TRACTOR IS ANGLED TO THE RIGHT OF THE TRAILER

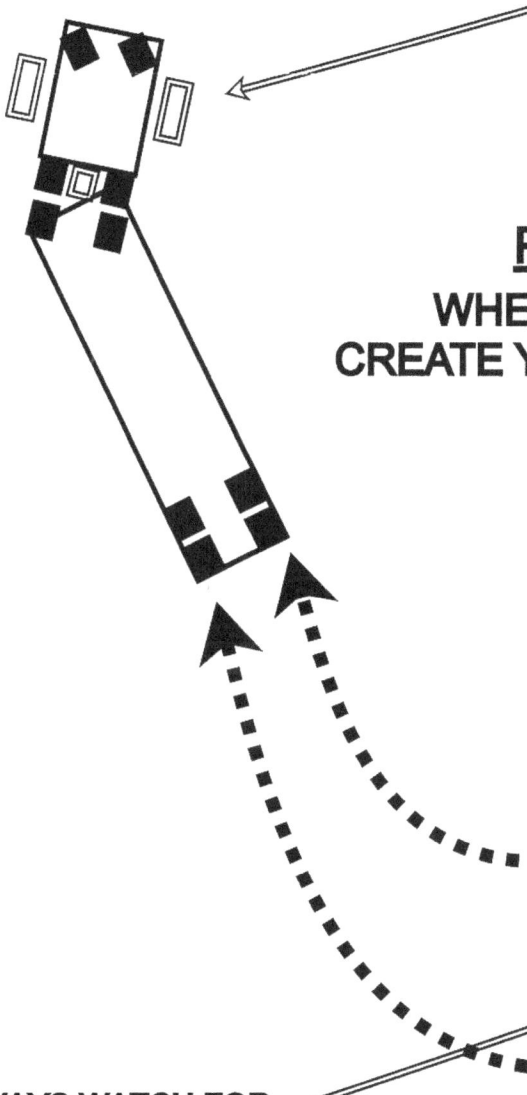

POINTS OF REFERENCE
WHEN THE CONDITIONS WARRANT, CREATE YOUR OWN POINTS OF REFERENCE

DRIVER'S REAR TANDEM POINTS OF REFERENCE

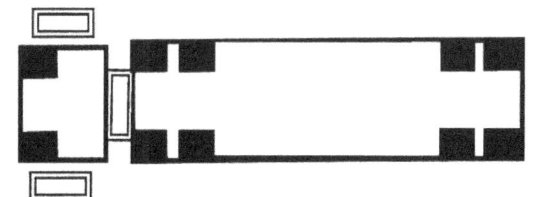

ALWAYS WATCH FOR HORIZONTAL SPACE

EXTREME CAUTION MUST BE TAKEN DUE TO VEHICLE BACKING ON DRIVER'S BLIND-SIDE, REGARDLESS OF TANDEMS POSITION.

OFFSET PARK:
LEFT TO RIGHT
WITH TANDEMS SLID BACK

THE TANDEMS AND THE BACK-END OF THE
TRAILER ARE CLOSE TO EACH OTHER.

FOLLOW THE PATH OF THE REAR TANDEMS,
AND THE BACK-END OF THE TRAILER
VERTICALLY AND HORIZONTALLY.

* ANTICIPATE THE "DELAY REACTION" *

* USE REFERENCE POINTS *

CONSTANTLY VIEW THE LEFT AND RIGHT
MIRRORS AS NEEDED.

AS THE LEFT REAR TANDEM IS JUST ABOUT TO ENTER THE HORIZONTAL SPACE,
TURN THE STEERING WHEEL MULTIPLE TURNS QUICKLY TO THE RIGHT THEN
LEFT, OR YOU CAN TURN THE STEERING WHEEL MULTIPLE TURNS QUICKLY
TO THE RIGHT THEN LEFT BY FOLLOWING THE RIGHT REAR TANDEM AND
REFERENCE POINT(S) ON THE RIGHT SIDE.

WHEN THE SPACE IS TIGHT, TURN
THE STEERING WHEEL BEFORE PULLING-UP.

OFFSET PARK: LEFT TO RIGHT

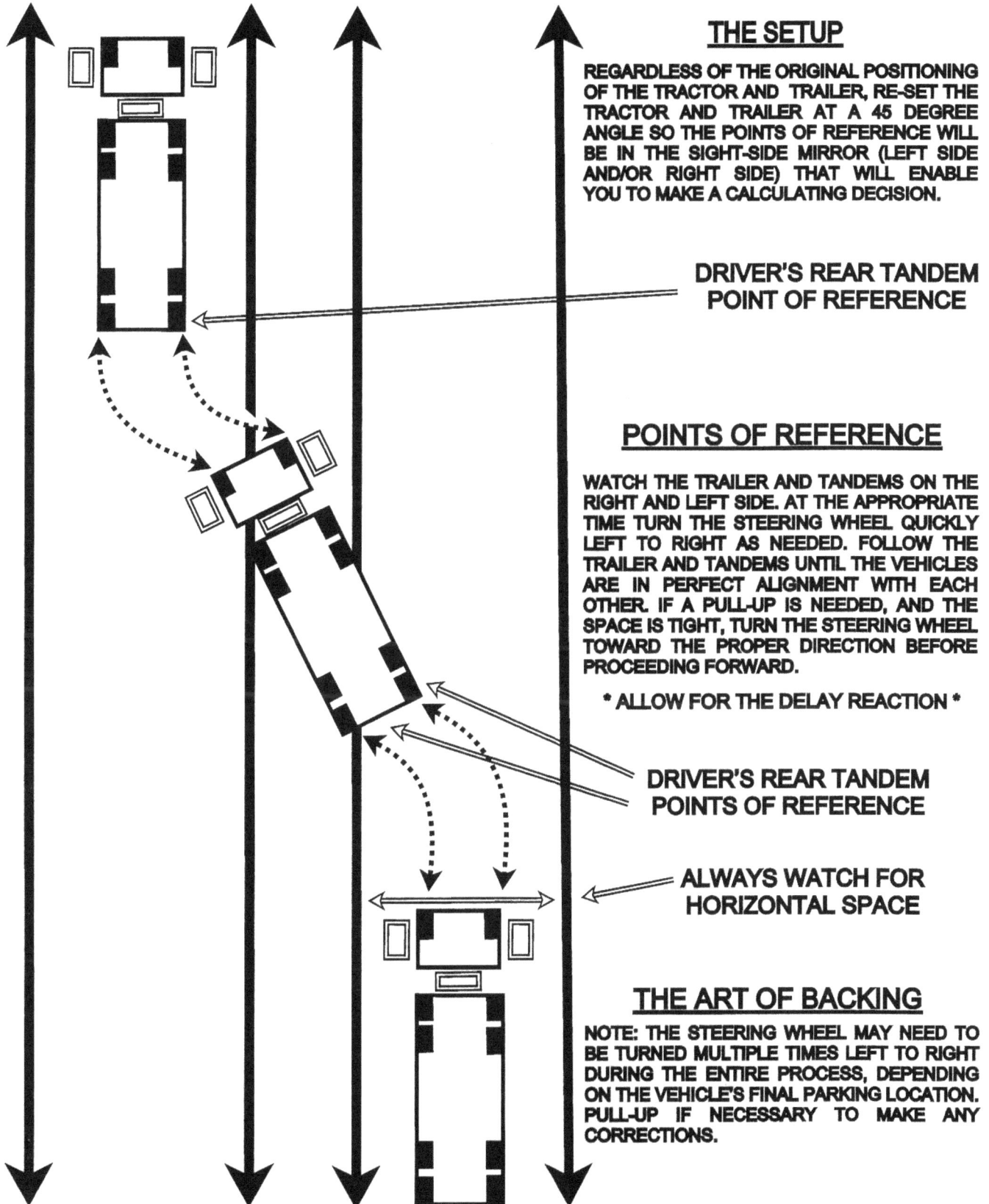

THE SETUP

REGARDLESS OF THE ORIGINAL POSITIONING OF THE TRACTOR AND TRAILER, RE-SET THE TRACTOR AND TRAILER AT A 45 DEGREE ANGLE SO THE POINTS OF REFERENCE WILL BE IN THE SIGHT-SIDE MIRROR (LEFT SIDE AND/OR RIGHT SIDE) THAT WILL ENABLE YOU TO MAKE A CALCULATING DECISION.

DRIVER'S REAR TANDEM POINT OF REFERENCE

POINTS OF REFERENCE

WATCH THE TRAILER AND TANDEMS ON THE RIGHT AND LEFT SIDE. AT THE APPROPRIATE TIME TURN THE STEERING WHEEL QUICKLY LEFT TO RIGHT AS NEEDED. FOLLOW THE TRAILER AND TANDEMS UNTIL THE VEHICLES ARE IN PERFECT ALIGNMENT WITH EACH OTHER. IF A PULL-UP IS NEEDED, AND THE SPACE IS TIGHT, TURN THE STEERING WHEEL TOWARD THE PROPER DIRECTION BEFORE PROCEEDING FORWARD.

* ALLOW FOR THE DELAY REACTION *

DRIVER'S REAR TANDEM POINTS OF REFERENCE

ALWAYS WATCH FOR HORIZONTAL SPACE

THE ART OF BACKING

NOTE: THE STEERING WHEEL MAY NEED TO BE TURNED MULTIPLE TIMES LEFT TO RIGHT DURING THE ENTIRE PROCESS, DEPENDING ON THE VEHICLE'S FINAL PARKING LOCATION. PULL-UP IF NECESSARY TO MAKE ANY CORRECTIONS.

OFFSET PARK:
RIGHT TO LEFT
WITH TANDEMS SLID BACK

THE TANDEMS AND THE BACK-END OF THE
TRAILER ARE CLOSE TO EACH OTHER.

FOLLOW THE PATH OF THE REAR TANDEMS,
AND THE BACK-END OF THE TRAILER
VERTICALLY AND HORIZONTALLY.

* ANTICIPATE THE "DELAY REACTION" *

* USE REFERENCE POINTS *

CONSTANTLY VIEW THE LEFT AND RIGHT
MIRRORS AS NEEDED.

AS THE RIGHT REAR TANDEM IS JUST ABOUT TO ENTER THE HORIZONTAL
SPACE, TURN THE STEERING WHEEL MULTIPLE TURNS QUICKLY TO THE LEFT
THEN RIGHT, OR YOU CAN TURN THE STEERING WHEEL MULTIPLE TURNS
QUICKLY TO THE LEFT THEN RIGHT BY FOLLOWING THE LEFT REAR TANDEM
AND REFERENCE POINT(S) ON THE LEFT SIDE.

WHEN THE SPACE IS TIGHT, TURN THE
STEERING WHEEL BEFORE PULLING-UP.

OFFSET PARK: RIGHT TO LEFT

THE SETUP

REGARDLESS OF THE ORIGINAL POSITIONING OF THE TRACTOR AND TRAILER, RE-SET THE TRACTOR AND TRAILER AT A 45 DEGREE ANGLE SO THE POINTS OF REFERENCE WILL BE IN THE SIGHT-SIDE MIRROR (LEFT SIDE AND/OR RIGHT SIDE) THAT WILL ENABLE YOU TO MAKE A CALCULATING DECISION.

DRIVER'S REAR TANDEM POINT OF REFERENCE

POINTS OF REFERENCE

WATCH THE TRAILER AND TANDEMS ON THE RIGHT AND LEFT SIDE. AT THE APPROPRIATE TIME TURN THE STEERING WHEEL QUICKLY RIGHT TO LEFT AS NEEDED. FOLLOW THE TRAILER AND TANDEMS UNTIL THE VEHICLES ARE IN PERFECT ALIGNMENT WITH EACH OTHER. IF A PULL-UP IS NEEDED, AND THE SPACE IS TIGHT, TURN THE STEERING WHEEL TOWARD THE PROPER DIRECTION BEFORE PROCEEDING FORWARD.

* ALLOW FOR THE DELAY REACTION *

DRIVER'S REAR TANDEM POINTS OF REFERENCE

ALWAYS WATCH FOR HORIZONTAL SPACE

THE ART OF BACKING

NOTE: THE STEERING WHEEL MAY NEED TO BE TURNED MULTIPLE TIMES RIGHT TO LEFT DURING THE ENTIRE PROCESS, DEPENDING ON THE VEHICLE'S FINAL PARKING LOCATION. PULL-UP IF NECESSARY TO MAKE ANY CORRECTIONS.

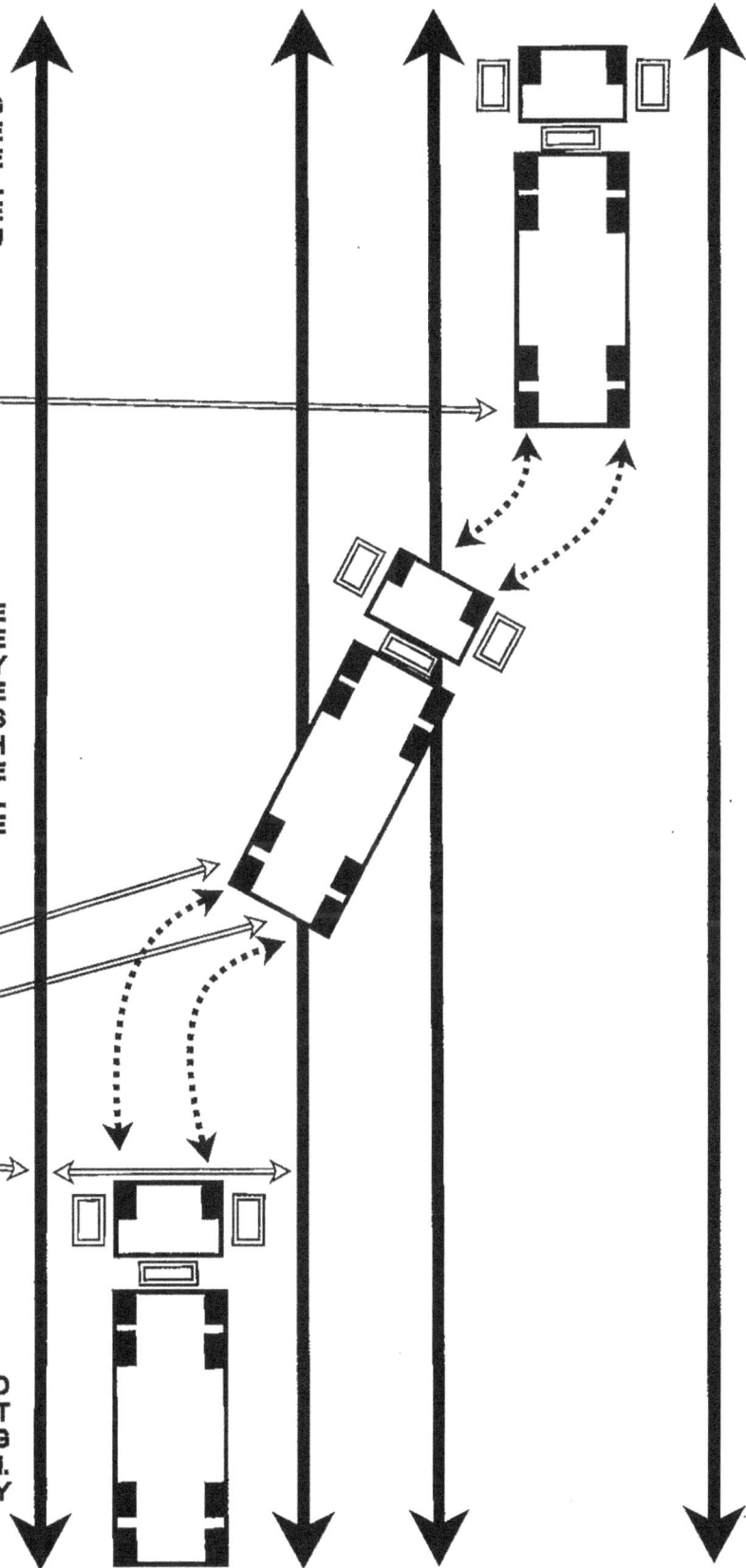

PARALLEL PARK:
LEFT TO RIGHT
WITH TANDEMS SLID BACK

THE TANDEMS AND THE BACK-END OF THE
TRAILER ARE CLOSE TO EACH OTHER.

FOLLOW THE PATH OF THE REAR TANDEMS,
AND THE BACK-END OF THE TRAILER
VERTICALLY AND HORIZONTALLY.

* ANTICIPATE THE "DELAY REACTION" *

* USE REFERENCE POINTS *

CONSTANTLY VIEW THE LEFT AND RIGHT
MIRRORS AS NEEDED.

AS THE LEFT REAR TANDEM IS JUST ABOUT TO ENTER THE HORIZONTAL SPACE,
TURN THE STEERING WHEEL MULTIPLE TURNS QUICKLY TO THE RIGHT THEN
LEFT, OR YOU CAN TURN THE STEERING WHEEL MULTIPLE TURNS QUICKLY
TO THE RIGHT THEN LEFT BY FOLLOWING THE RIGHT REAR TANDEM AND
REFERENCE POINT(S) ON THE RIGHT SIDE.

WHEN THE SPACE IS TIGHT, TURN THE
STEERING WHEEL BEFORE PULLING-UP.

PARALLEL PARK: LEFT TO RIGHT

THE SETUP

REGARDLESS OF THE ORIGINAL POSITIONING OF THE TRACTOR AND TRAILER, RE-SET THE TRACTOR AND TRAILER AT A 45 DEGREE ANGLE SO THE POINTS OF REFERENCE WILL BE IN THE SIGHT-SIDE MIRROR (LEFT SIDE AND/OR RIGHT SIDE) THAT WILL ENABLE YOU TO MAKE A CALCULATING DECISION.

POINTS OF REFERENCE

WATCH THE TRAILER AND TANDEMS ON THE LEFT AND RIGHT SIDE. AT THE APPROPRIATE TIME TURN THE STEERING WHEEL QUICKLY LEFT TO RIGHT AS NEEDED. FOLLOW THE TRAILER AND TANDEMS UNTIL THE VEHICLES ARE IN PERFECT ALIGNMENT WITH EACH OTHER. IF A PULL-UP IS NEEDED, AND THE SPACE IS TIGHT, TURN THE STEERING WHEEL TOWARD THE PROPER DIRECTION BEFORE PROCEEDING FORWARD.

* ALLOW FOR THE DELAY REACTION *

DRIVER'S REAR TANDEM
POINTS OF REFERENCE

ALWAYS WATCH FOR
HORIZONTAL SPACE

THE ART OF BACKING

NOTE: THE STEERING WHEEL MAY NEED TO BE TURNED MULTIPLE TIMES LEFT TO RIGHT, DURING THE ENTIRE PROCESS, DEPENDING ON THE VEHICLE'S FINAL PARKING LOCATION. PULL-UP IF NECESSARY TO MAKE ANY CORRECTIONS.

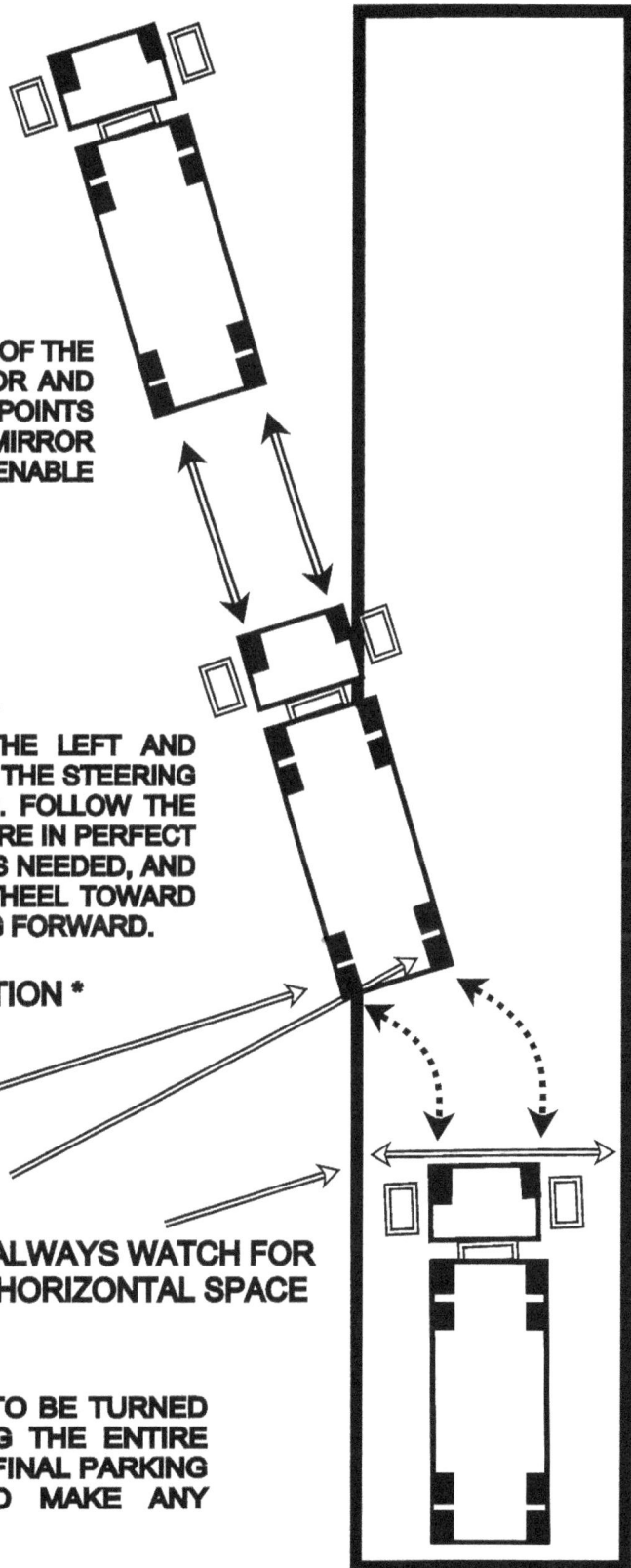

PARALLEL PARK:
RIGHT TO LEFT
WITH TANDEMS SLID BACK

THE TANDEMS AND THE BACK-END OF THE TRAILER ARE CLOSE TO EACH OTHER.

FOLLOW THE PATH OF THE REAR TANDEMS, AND THE BACK-END OF THE TRAILER VERTICALLY AND HORIZONTALLY.

* ANTICIPATE THE "DELAY REACTION" *

* USE REFERENCE POINTS *

CONSTANTLY VIEW THE LEFT AND RIGHT MIRRORS AS NEEDED.

AS THE RIGHT REAR TANDEM IS JUST ABOUT TO ENTER THE HORIZONTAL SPACE, TURN THE STEERING WHEEL MULTIPLE TURNS QUICKLY TO THE LEFT THEN RIGHT, OR YOU CAN TURN THE STEERING WHEEL MULTIPLE TURNS QUICKLY TO THE LEFT THEN RIGHT BY FOLLOWING THE LEFT REAR TANDEM AND REFERENCE POINT(S) ON THE LEFT SIDE.

WHEN THE SPACE IS TIGHT, TURN THE STEERING WHEEL BEFORE PULLING-UP.

PARALLEL PARK: RIGHT TO LEFT

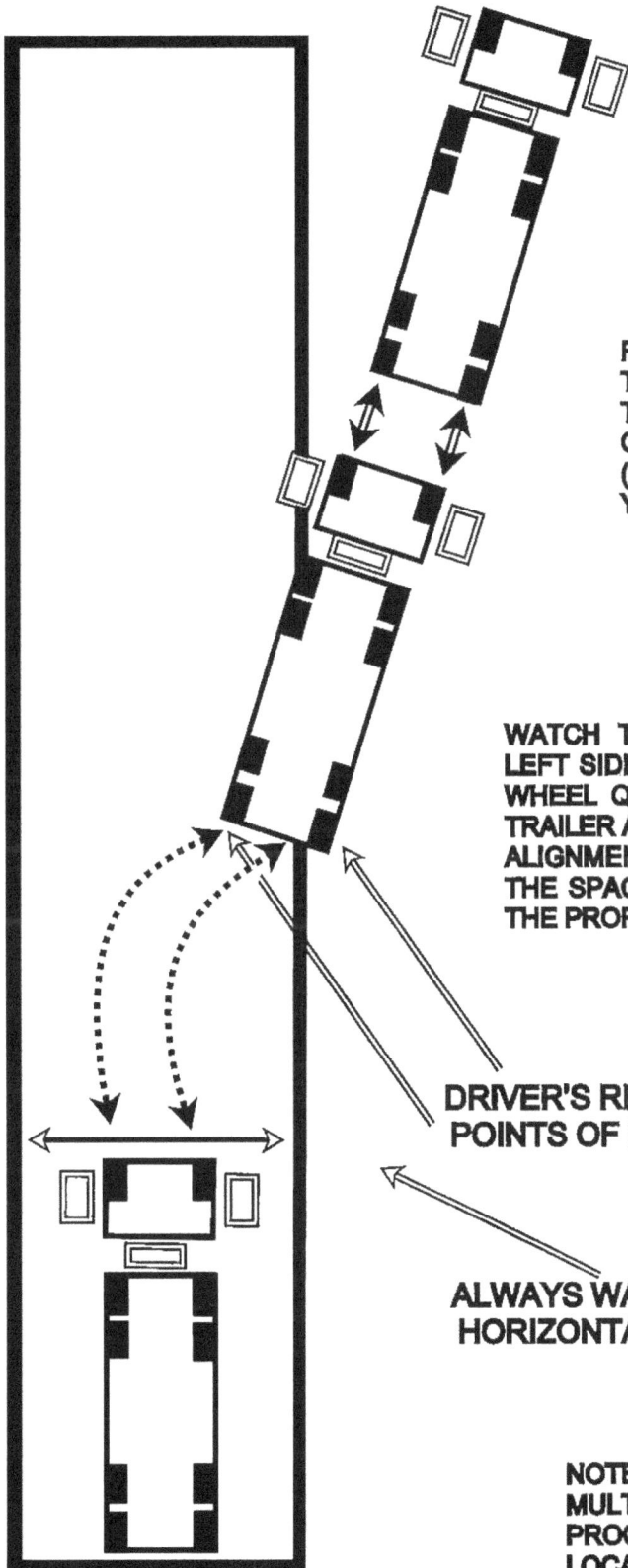

THE SETUP

REGARDLESS OF THE ORIGINAL POSITIONING OF THE TRACTOR AND TRAILER, RE-SET THE TRACTOR AND TRAILER AT A 45 DEGREE ANGLE SO THE POINTS OF REFERENCE WILL BE IN THE SIGHT-SIDE MIRROR (LEFT SIDE AND/OR RIGHT SIDE) THAT WILL ENABLE YOU TO MAKE A CALCULATING DECISION.

POINTS OF REFERENCE

WATCH THE TRAILER AND TANDEMS ON THE RIGHT AND LEFT SIDE. AT THE APPROPRIATE TIME TURN THE STEERING WHEEL QUICKLY RIGHT TO LEFT AS NEEDED. FOLLOW THE TRAILER AND TANDEMS UNTIL THE VEHICLES ARE IN PERFECT ALIGNMENT WITH EACH OTHER. IF A PULL-UP IS NEEDED, AND THE SPACE IS TIGHT, TURN THE STEERING WHEEL TOWARD THE PROPER DIRECTION BEFORE PROCEEDING FORWARD.

* ALLOW FOR THE DELAY REACTION *

DRIVER'S REAR TANDEM
POINTS OF REFERENCE

ALWAYS WATCH FOR
HORIZONTAL SPACE

THE ART OF BACKING

NOTE: THE STEERING WHEEL MAY NEED TO BE TURNED MULTIPLE TIMES RIGHT TO LEFT, DURING THE ENTIRE PROCESS, DEPENDING ON THE VEHICLE'S FINAL PARKING LOCATION. PULL-UP IF NECESSARY TO MAKE ANY CORRECTIONS.

SIGHT-SIDE
ALLEY DOCK
WITH TANDEMS SLID BACK
TIGHT HORIZONTAL SPACE

THE <u>TANDEMS</u> AND THE <u>BACK-END</u> OF THE
<u>TRAILER</u> <u>ARE</u> <u>CLOSE</u> TO <u>EACH</u> <u>OTHER.</u>

MOVE THE <u>TANDEMS</u> <u>FORWARD</u>, <u>DEPENDING</u>
ON <u>"HOW</u> <u>TIGHT"</u> THE <u>HORIZONTAL</u> SPACE IS.
<u>ALWAYS</u> BE <u>AWARE</u> OF THE <u>TRAILER</u> <u>OVERHANG.</u>

<u>FOLLOW</u> THE <u>FRONT</u> OF THE <u>CAB</u>, THE <u>PATH</u> OF THE <u>REAR</u>
<u>TANDEMS</u>, AND THE <u>BACK-END</u> OF THE <u>TRAILER</u>
<u>VERTICALLY</u> AND <u>HORIZONTALLY.</u>

* <u>ANTICIPATE</u> <u>THE</u> <u>"DELAY</u> <u>REACTION"</u> *

* <u>USE</u> <u>REFERENCE</u> <u>POINTS</u> *

<u>CONSTANTLY</u> <u>VIEW</u> THE <u>LEFT</u> AND <u>RIGHT</u>
<u>MIRRORS</u> AS <u>NEEDED.</u>

<u>TURN</u> THE <u>STEERING</u> <u>WHEEL</u> <u>QUICKLY</u>, <u>ALWAYS</u>
<u>FOLLOWING</u> THE <u>PATH</u> OF THE <u>REAR</u> <u>TANDEMS</u>,
AND THE <u>BACK-END</u> OF THE <u>TRAILER.</u>

WHEN THE SPACE IS <u>TIGHT</u>, TURN
THE STEERING WHEEL <u>BEFORE</u> PULLING-UP.

SIGHT-SIDE ALLEY DOCK
WITH TANDEMS SLID BACK
TIGHT HORIZONTAL SPACE WITH BUILDINGS, HOMES, ETC.

THE SETUP

THE TIGHTER THE AVAILABLE SPACE, THE MORE IMPORTANT IT IS TO PROPERLY SETUP.

DECISION TIME

SLIDE THE TANDEMS FORWARD AS NEEDED. THE TIGHTER THE HORIZONTAL SPACE, THE MORE THE TANDEMS NEED TO BE SLID FORWARD.

MULTI-TASK

WATCH LEFT AND RIGHT SIDE OF THE TRAILER, WHILE SIMULTANEOUSLY WATCHING THE SWING OF THE TRACTOR.

ALWAYS WATCH FOR THE HORIZONTAL SPACE IN FRONT AS TRACTOR SWINGS RIGHT

ALWAYS WATCH FOR HORIZONTAL SPACE

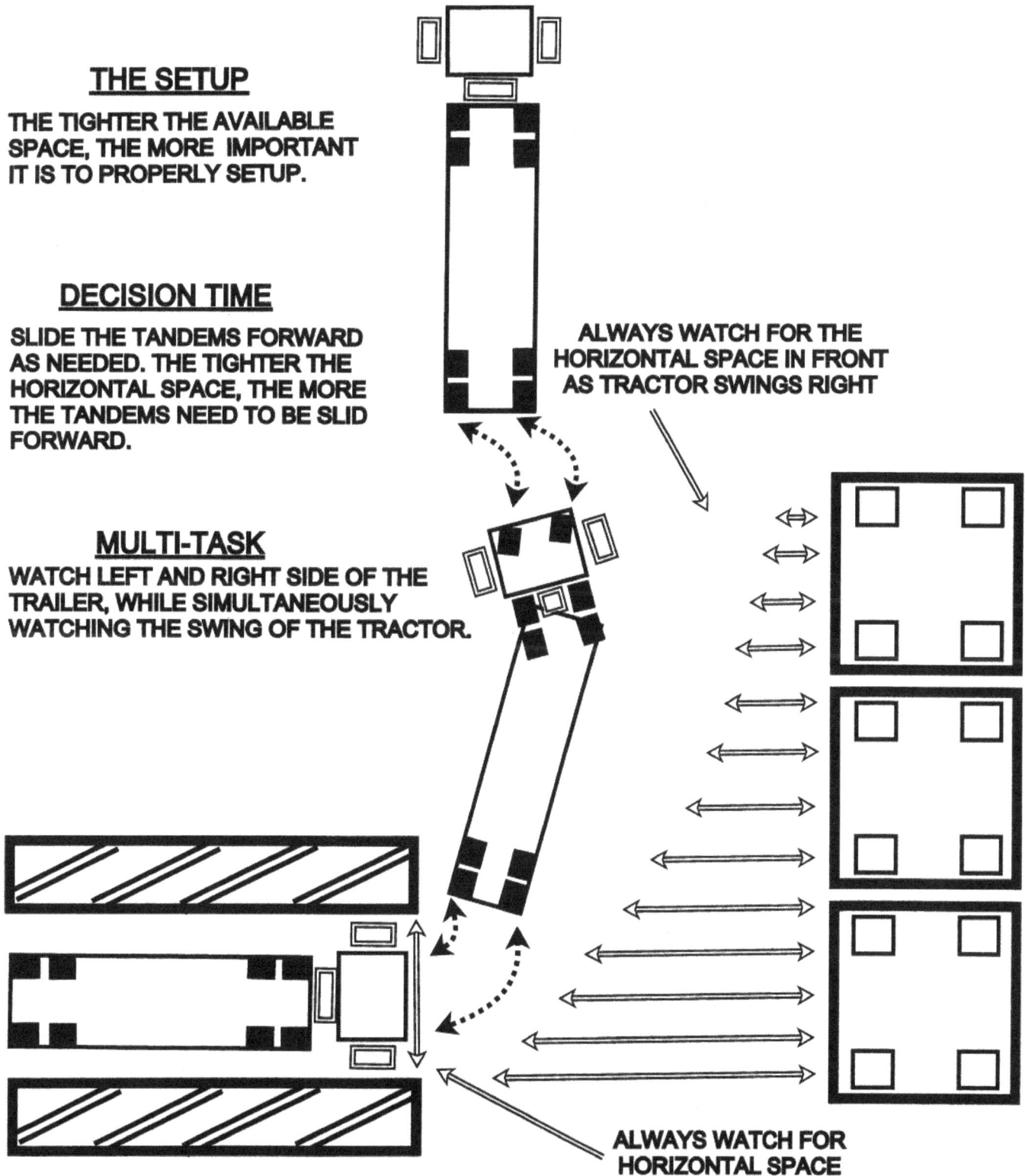

Getting Good Directions is Critical

All Directions are Not Created Equal

Plan Your Trip in Advance, or Else

The most important thing you can, and should, do as a professional driver never having previously been to a specific destination for a pick-up or drop, is to **plan your trip in advance.**

As difficult and frustrating as it is to be lost when driving a car, a **multiplier *of* ten** can be added when you are lost driving a tractor-trailer. For example:

- There may not be any viable street to turn around that is in the general vicinity of where you presently are at in order to get to where you want to go. Getting lost is nerve-wracking. Depending on the severity of the time frame, being lost will cause any number of the following problems:

- **Aggravation** to the point of having an accident due to the stress of the situation.

- **Arriving late** to your destination, causing you to possibly arrive late at your next pick-up or drop as well. And so forth.

- **An unhappy customer** needing their freight picked up or dropped off. Should they operate in a J.I.T mode (Just-In-Time). this can become a very serious logistical and financial problem for all parties involved.

- **The Consignee or Consignor.** They may have to deal with how to solve the issue of a late delivery that can have a detrimental effect on their customer's, as well as the repercussions on the business.

- **The Trucking Company.** Not meeting the customer's requirements equates to an unhappy employer who may lose the customer to another trucking company, or pay a late delivery fine.
- **Your Very Unhappy Dispatcher/Driver Manager/Fleet Manager.** This person and/or people **expect** and **depend** on the professional driver to meet their obligations.
- **The Driver.** Due to being late, the company may be closed for the night. Being stuck at the location for the morning or over the weekend is a disastrous situation for everyone involved. This may cause your drops and pick-ups for the run to be late, and you may not be able to leave for your backhaul as scheduled. A substitute driver may have to be found.
- **Note:** When it is not realistic to meet an arranged time-frame (due to circumstances beyond your control), **immediately** contact the appropriate person according to company policy.

The Other Side of the Coin

As disastrous as the above scenarios can be, **IF** you plan your trip properly in advance (especially if you have never been to that destination before) your trip can be a **pleasure.** It is critical you know the **proper directions** pertaining to the **exact streets** you need to be driving on, in order to arrive on time and safe.

GPS for the Tractor-Trailer

Should you choose to go high tech, be certain to **ONLY** purchase a GPS that has the proper software written for a **tractor-trailer.** The standard GPS system designed for the automobile is useless. It does not account for, and is not designed for, the physical difference between a tractor-trailer and an automobile. GPS software can provide you with information about specific things such as those listed below, if you purchase a quality unit. However, as of this writing, there is no GPS on the market that is foolproof. Be certain to update the software as required. Extreme caution is **ALWAYS** warranted as the GPS may not be giving you the information you need.

Benefits of Having a GPS:

- Notice of low viaducts forthcoming
- Streets you should not be on (too narrow, etc.)
- Construction updates
- Notification of scales

- Traffic updates
- Speed limit changes
- Address book software

One Possible Disadvantage of the GPS

- The GPS May Not Always Provide the Shortest Route

Trucker's Atlas

Important: Even if you decide to purchase a high quality GPS unit, it will be in your best-interest to **ALWAYS** have the standard Trucker's Atlas that can be purchased at truck stops throughout the country. They may be considered old fashioned and obsolete by some, and cumbersome by others however, the Trucker's Atlas has a proven track record.

A high quality Trucker's Atlas will provide you with an immense amount of information literally, from A to Z. This accolade is not to say a high tech GPS is not good to purchase. Own both if you wish, but **ALWAYS** keep a professional Trucker's Atlas in your vehicle, as well. You never know when you just may need it.

THE TRUCKER'S ATLAS IS WORTH IT'S WEIGHT IN GOLD

Calling the Consignee and Consignor

There are times it becomes necessary to actually place a phone call to the company you will be driving to for any of the following reasons, and more:

- Directions
- Their normal operating hours
- Pick-up and delivery appointment times
- Skeleton hours of operation for holidays
- If you have knowledge of information such as inclement weather in their vicinity, it can very well be worth a quick phone call to be certain they will be open when you get there.

The major reason for calling a company prior to arriving is generally for directions. It is very important to obtain the best directions you possibly can. Knowing the proper, most expeditious way to arrive at the location of a customer is the difference between a pleasant trip and one that will bring you nothing but aggravation.

- Be certain to ask for the details you need.
- Listen very carefully.
- Write the directions down, or use a recording device.
- Ask the person you are speaking with to repeat if it's necessary.
- If you are not receiving good information from the person: **Ask politely** to speak to another person. Perhaps the first person on the phone is not really certain what the best route is for you to take, **or** it may be they are in a rush themselves and don't have the patience to spend a few minutes of their time to help you.

In most cases, the need for good directions is required as soon as you get off an interstate highway. The following are some methods to consider:

- First and foremost: You must let the person you are speaking with know you are driving a tractor-trailer. This can be very significant when low bridges, narrow streets, etc. are in the play.
- Know which direction you are arriving from: North, South, East or West. This is **very important.**
- Always ask for the interstate number you will be getting off at. Ask if that interstate number covers two or more exits, A, B or C. Each exit will have different information.
- Ask for the information written on the interstate sign in addition to the number, such as a street name, a specific route number, or a major destination spot such as a sporting venue, restaurant, etc.
- Ask for the proper way to proceed after getting off the exit.
- Ask about the signs immediately after you exit (stop sign, possibly a four way, yield sign, standard stop lights, flashing yellow light, flashing red light, etc.)
- Ask which way to turn (left turn, right turn, etc.)
- Ask for points of reference that can be easily and quickly be seen along the direction route such as: Restaurants, car washes, churches, special landmarks, etc. This is very important, because the person you are speaking with may say something to you such as: "Go up the street six or seven miles." Don't take the six or seven miles as gospel. They may be off by three miles, and you may find yourself confused, and/or end up going past the street you need to turn onto.
- Ask if there is a light (standard/flashing) on the corner of the street you are turning onto.
- Ask for a landmark at the specific corner you are turning onto. A restaurant, used car lot, etc. You are now getting **very close** to your destination point.
- Be certain to ask for the **exact entrance** you need to **enter safely.** Again, the person you are speaking with **must know** you are arriving in a **tractor-trailer.**

Save Your Directions

By saving the directions, starting with the exit number, and including sign information from the interstate or other major road, you will be storing valuable information for the future, that will make your life as a professional driver considerably easier and more pleasurable. Unless you have a dedicated run on a continual basis, you could end up with hundreds or thousands of pick-ups and/or drops.

> ## THE DIFFICULTY IN REMEMBERING EVERY TURN *AND* NUANCE TO ARRIVE ON TIME AND SAFELY CAN BE OVERWHELMING.

Make your life easier for the future by storing the information. Write it into a notebook, or use a 3 x 5 file card system, or go high tech. It does not matter, as long as you maintain the information for the future. Not only can memory fade as time goes by, but surroundings look quite different during daylight as compared to evening hours, and you **never know** when you will need to make a future drop at any of these same locations.

A few important considerations to take into account for the need to save directions are:

- **An extended time-frame** of not being at the customer's location can cloud your memory as to the numerous rights and lefts, etc. you need to remember in order to arrive **safely, on time** with **minimal stress.**

- **Daylight driving vs. night-time driving** can confuse anyone, as everything begins to look different as the sun goes down.

A Word of Caution:

- **Low Bridges**

     Anytime a person tells you to go under a bridge, viaduct, or whatever other possible forthcoming obstacle, **immediately state you are in a tractor-trailer.** They may not know (or they may not be thinking about) this important fact. Ask if there is enough height to pass through. **Do not** take it for granted they know you are driving a tractor-trailer.

- **Rotaries, Roundabouts, and Circles**

     Throughout the country there are configurations that are not necessarily commonplace. The northeastern states have more rotaries, roundabouts, and circles than any other parts of the country. The difference between a rotary, roundabout or a circle is technical in the method of the traffic flow. Some circles and roundabouts are generally smaller and configured more efficiently than older rotaries that can be quite large. Almost all rotaries are large in size. The important thing to know is how to drive safely around them. The largest number of these configurations will be found in the northeast, specifically in Massachusetts, where they seem to be endless.

- **Entering and Driving Safely Around the Rotary**

Should you be familiar with the rotary, you have the distinct advantage of knowing which lane is appropriate to be in. If this is not the case, proceed cautiously and be prepared to possibly drive around more than once in order to move over toward the proper lane that will take you to your exit. Watch for other vehicles as there may very well be other drivers in your same convoluted situation.

Don't Depend on the CB Radio

On occasion, you will hear from a truck driver who will state they like to wait until they get within what they **"hope"** is just a few miles of their pickup or drop. Then you will be told they like to get on the **"horn"** and ask if anyone in the area knows how to get to "ABC Company." **This is not only old school, but it's foolish and dangerous.** Be a professional, do it right, and march to the beat of your own drummer.

CB radios can serve a very useful purpose, and it is suggested every professional driver own one. However, there is a proper time and place to use your CB.

Asking for Help

Life is not perfect, neither are driving directions. Should you find yourself in a quandary, and you have the opportunity to safely pull over - **do it!** The people living and working in the area may be able to help you. The list can be endless:

- Police department
- Fire department
- Local police officer working his or her beat in the area
- DOT officer working in the area
- A local merchant